DEPRESSED TO
DARING

DEPRESSED TO DARING

Channel your inner superwoman.
Defeat anxiety and depression, and gain
control over your life and career.

ADONICA SHAW

This book contains information, anecdotes, and advice relating to mental health, wellness, and health care. This information should not be used or leveraged in lieu of medical or psychiatric advice, care, or guidance. Please consult with a medical professional before embarking on any program or course of treatment for mental illness. The publisher, author, and editors disclaim liability for any medical or psychiatric outcomes that may occur as a result of applying the methods discussed in this book.

The names and identifying details of the people and situations discussed herein have been changed or omitted to protect their privacy.

Copyright 2020 by Adonica Shaw. All rights reserved. Printed in the United States of America. No part of this book may be used or reproduced in any manner whatsoever without written permission except in the case of brief quotations embodied in critical articles or reviews.

Library of Congress Control Number: 2020901275

ISBN 978-0-578-63421-0 (Hardcover)
ISBN 978-0-578-63944-4 (Paperback)
ISBN 978-1-0878-1833-7 (ebook)

Cover design by Vanessa Mendozzi
Author Photograph by Crystal Lee

First Edition

*For every woman who has had to overcome
herself to find out who she really is.*

"You either walk inside your story and own it, or you stand outside your story and hustle for your worthiness."

— Brené Brown

Contents

Author's Note ix
Introduction xii
    What to Expect: xviii
    How to use what you are learning: xix

CHAPTER ONE BE AGILE, NOT FRAGILE 1
    The Anatomy of Agility-Driven Behavior 5
    Putting Emotional Agility into Practice 9
    In Case No One Has Told You: 12

CHAPTER TWO TRANSFORM YOUR TRANSACTIONS 13
    Thoughts are Emotional Transactions 17
    Quality Over Quantity 19
    Use "Spend. Give. Save." Decide What to Focus on 20
    Putting "Spend. Give. Save" into Practice 21
    Leverage Your Attention Strategically 22
    Transforming How You Think 24
    In Case No One Has Told You 25

CHAPTER THREE MIND YOUR GAP 26
    Your Beliefs are Just Thoughts You Keep Thinking 29
    Mind Your Gap 29
    What are Emotional Triggers? 30
    Get Real 31
    Put it into Practice. Track Your Triggers 33
    In Case No One Has Told You 36

CHAPTER FOUR SURRENDER TO SELF-CARE 37
- Self-Care 101 40
- Boundaries, Boundaries, Boundaries 41
- Get Radical about Self-Care 49
- In Case No One Has Told You: 58

CHAPTER FIVE ALIGN TO CLIMB 59
- What Does Alignment Look Like? 63
- How Do I Know if I'm Out of Alignment? 64
- Your Gut Gives Guidance 65
- Align to Level Up 66
- In Case No One Has Told You: 71

Chapter SIX PURGE TO RE-EMERGE 72
- Therapy 76
- What to Look for in a Good Therapist or Counselor 82
- Surrender Circles 84
- Verbal Vomit Exercises 85
- In Case No One Has Told You: 88

In Conclusion 89
Acknowledgements 91
About the Author 92

AUTHOR'S NOTE

I wrote *Depressed to Daring* to help women discover the power of emotional agility and radical self-care, and how these things can dramatically improve the quality of their personal and professional lives.

On the surface, we all know that our mental and emotional health should be a priority, but unfortunately, for working moms, women in high-stakes careers, and others who are just trying to achieve balance in their professional and financial lives, such matters take a back seat due to cyclical patterns and longstanding habits.

As women, we are constantly creating this image in our minds about what our life should look like, and how we want to be perceived. Many of us are quick to create a list of things we want to accomplish within the next thirty, sixty or ninety days, but forget about the time, expertise, and experience it takes to acquire the life we want to live.

That's where this book comes in. It's meant to offer practical advice and information that you can use to build your emotional muscles and mental strength.

I'll be discussing the concept of emotional agility and how it empowered me during some of my most difficult life experiences. Prior to leveraging this skill, I was always caught in cycles of anxiety and depression whenever stressful events

Depressed to Daring

arose in my life. For years, this made it difficult to have a firm grasp on my emotional health, let alone remain grounded in high-pressure environments.

Now, I can tell you that the details of my journey are unique only to me, my personal life, and decisions I made along the way, but the truth is, I'm not unlike most women.

Women who want to be the epitome of success (domestically and professionally) to other women.

Women who have always aspired to be in leadership positions.

Women who have at one point or another desired a perfect family with the perfect spouse.

Women who want to uphold their family reputation through their achievements.

Women who want to establish a solid professional reputation in their local communities.

Women who want to be the mother to their children that they never had.

Women who want to be known for our ability to shoulder stress effortlessly in male-dominated environments.

Women who want to outwork or outperform female competitors in their respective fields.

Depressed to Daring

Women who use alcohol to cope with life's stresses, and act as if this habit is providing balance when it's doing anything but.

Women who have always wanted to do something unique and grandiose with their life but lacked the support system necessary to help them achieve success and maintain emotional balance as they learn to manage the stress triggers that come with high levels of responsibility.

I want to be upfront by telling you that there is no expectation for you to read this and to adopt every piece of information in these pages. Take what resonates, and leave the rest for another day, or perhaps as friendly advice to another woman you know.

If you're ready to take control over your life and become a stronger, more balanced version of yourself, read on.

INTRODUCTION

You are a daring, powerful, confident woman.

The summer of 2018 was a turning point in my life. I was on the verge of bankruptcy, recovering from surgery, and battling exorbitant amounts of stress that, on my worst days, left me overwhelmed, anxious, and living in fear that the dreams I had for myself would never see the light of day. I was also working at all hours to expand my professional network, in addition to raising three kids with my then-spouse.

Outwardly, I was poised, gracious, and put together, but on the inside, I was despondent and anxiety-ridden because I didn't have a practical plan to balance everything. I was torn about opening up to friends, and I was on the fence about going to a life coach because for me, at that time, getting coached seemed to imply that I wasn't strong enough to shoulder the load I was begging to carry.

I couldn't fathom paying a complete stranger to tell me how to act or how to live on a daily basis. And though I had always been comfortable with the idea of self-help, new-age gurus, the thought of actually paying someone my hard-earned money to organize my life seemed absolutely absurd. So, I turned to my network of mommy friends and colleagues. These powerful women were thought leaders, business owners, and innovators, who, in my eyes, had learned the secret to balancing everything. Clearly, they had some nugget of advice I could use, right?

Well, not exactly.

There were many days I remember calling friends just to catch up. After passing through the usual conversational checkpoints of family life and school projects, I would find a way to pivot to a not-so-small problem I was facing in hopes that they would tell me what to do next. Honestly, even though they tried their best to offer support and advice, most of the conversations ended politely with, "You're the smartest person I know. I'm sure you'll figure it out." The more this happened, the more frustrated I grew. With all of the blogs, podcasts, and social media gurus, it seemed that someone must have been able to offer me practical advice. I knew I couldn't be the only woman struggling to figure out how in the hell they were supposed to manage their family, finances, and career aspirations without going crazy. Nonetheless, my response was always laced with confidence: "You're probably right. I've figured things out a million times before."

To my friends' credit, though, I had figured things out before. I had all of the accoutrements of success; I had been a scholarship Division I athlete, a pageant winner, a weatherwoman, a TEDx speaker, a business owner, a community leader, and I had even run for office. At the same time, however, there were still aspects of my life that I desperately needed to change. There was information that I was lacking that was making it difficult to ascend even further than where I was, and I didn't exactly know how to go about getting it, in an - *I don't want to expose myself for not knowing what I don't know and don't want to be judged, shamed, or blamed for how I've done things in the past or how I think I should do them now* - kind of way.

You see, in my hidden world of high-functioning, millennial, do-it-all women, I developed this habit of curbing my conversation just enough to and omit any piece of information that could be used against me in social circles. The goal was always to protect my disciplined, picture-perfect persona. I learned very early in my career, by watching the downfall of some of my most admired colleagues and friends, that in most cases I would actually "figure it out," and the risky proposition of exposing the truth—that I was struggling to balance it all—wasn't worth the potential exclusion from professional or social opportunities.

I was conflicted by the inner knowledge that I needed to protect my reputation and the fact that I wasn't showing up for my life in the way I knew I could—that I wasn't doing enough to deal with where I was, so I could get to where I wanted to go.

I had a deep awareness that I could have anything, be anyone, and accomplish anything. I believed I had the power to be a daring, powerful, confident woman if I put my heart into it. I knew there had to be something more to my life than juggling stress and getting ahead. But, whenever I would get dangerously close to any solution that could have possibly revealed too much about myself, I withdrew. I figured I had time to figure it out on my own terms.

Let's just say, the universe had other plans.

Depressed to Daring

I wish I could tell you that I figured things out that summer, but that wouldn't be true. I tried all of the tricks and tropes I had seen other professional women use, where they evade the truth, tuck away their misfortune, and even deny themselves a new life by maintaining the status quo, but none of it worked.

In fact, the more I tried to grasp the life I had so carefully designed, the harsher the response from the universe proved. What I came to learn that season is that the universe, however you want to frame this for yourself, is always gently guiding us to the path of least resistance. It is always guiding us to the path of authentic power. When we accept the nudges of insight that are given to us to help us clean up our act, things move much more smoothly. What most often happens, though, is that our ego steps in, and we try to hide, evade, protect, or eclipse anything we feel is a threat to our personal control. And while it may work in certain seasons in your early life, it will not work as you try to ascend higher into the ranks of personal, professional, political, or spiritual success. By holding on to outdated thinking, not only do you become stressed, overwhelmed and depressed, but you also build undue tolerance for that which must be let go to make room for positive change.

The way this manifested for me was that, by trying to hold on, certain opportunities were passed up for others because I didn't have the emotional and mental skill set to manage what I was calling into my life. As a result, my personal and professional reputation suffered.

The most interesting thing I recognized while all of this was happening was the disproportionate amount of resources that teach women how to climb to success versus the ones that teach us how to stay there or to ascend when, through our own resistance or ego, we don't quite know how to traverse the glass ceilings we set for ourselves through our emotional and mental habits.

If you've picked up this book, there's a good chance that you've plateaued in some area of your life, and due to your inability to manage your current situation or plan for the future, your mental health is suffering. You probably know you can do a hell of a lot better than you're doing right now . . . provided the right information.

If this is you, then you're correct. I would also take it a step further by stating that you may need to shift your whole belief system. Wanting change isn't enough. We must commit to the behavior that will illuminate our lives.

This might be an uncomfortable change because, as you begin to change your habits, you're inevitably going to change the trajectory of your life. The roles and opportunities will be different. Your friend circle will change. Your habits and tastes in activities will shift. Hell, you may not even view dating and committed relationships the same way as you used to.

But you know what? It's worth it—and, girl, it feels amazing! I don't know what has happened or is about to unfold in your life, but whether you're going through some difficult shit or starting over after overcoming some difficult shit, the information in this book is equally valid.

A radical shakeup was what I needed to get my rear into gear, stop making excuses, and do the work. And by doing so,

Depressed to Daring

I built the grit and the character I needed to navigate from the darkest, most depressing days of my past to the brilliant, exuberant, joy-filled moments my present life entails.

This book is about becoming your best self, despite dealing with anxiety, stress, and depression. We're going to learn about skills like emotional agility, self-care, and rigorous honesty to build confidence and self-empowerment.

My dedication to living this way has changed every area of my life. I've been able to bring my life into balance. I have learned to let go of codependent behavior that kept me reliant on the validation of others. My fear-based thinking, insecurities, and feelings of inadequacy also lightened. I now see obstacles in my personal and professional environments as opportunities to develop more emotional muscle.

I've learned that I really am the key to my own success and that I'm responsible for honestly seeking the wisdom I need to maintain my inner strength. There's a quote from Joan Didion which reads, "The willingness to accept responsibility for one's own life is the source from which self-respect springs." This has never rung truer. While I, as the writer of this book, except that I'm an ever-evolving work in progress, I also acknowledge that the door to that knowledge is self-accountability and self-responsibility. It is my educated guess that if you've picked up this book, you are open to experiencing the same in yourself as well.

As you develop your own sense of emotional groundedness, you too will begin to improve the quality of your thoughts and mental state. Your mindset is the stage for any action you take. By learning how to use it more effectively, you can greatly improve the trajectory of your life.

What to Expect:

This book is divided into several chapters. Each chapter contains a principle for you to learn and practical information. You'll also find quotes, words of encouragement, and questions to consider sprinkled throughout the book. The exercises herein can be completed alone or discussed with a group.

Chapter 1: Be Agile, Not Fragile

Believe it or not, you do not have to offer an emotional response to every situation you find yourself in. This chapter offers the working definitions of emotional agility and emotional groundedness that are the foundation of this book.

Chapter 2: Transform your Transactions

Your energy is an investment. This chapter is all about the concept of managing your emotions like currency. You'll be guided to see the value in your emotions and how you can learn to invest them into the people, places, and things that will mutually invest in you.

Chapter 3: Mind Your Gap

Are you set off by any and everything during the day? This chapter will help you identify your triggers so you can manage them better on a day to day basis.

Chapter 4: Surrender to Self-Care

Do you know what self-care is? Do you know why you have to provide it on a regular basis? This chapter discusses the emerging trend of scheduling time for yourself to do nothing but examine yourself and explore the things that excite you.

Chapter 5: Align to Climb

I'll guide you through the concept of alignment and what that looks like in your habits. You'll learn a few tips and tricks to maintain your balance when something unexpected comes your way.

Chapter 6: Purge to Re-emerge

You'll learn that by purging or talking to a friend, community or therapist, it will become easier to manage the weight of your life. Though the idea of therapy is notably taboo for the silent generation, it is being popularized by women of all types in today's world. We are going to get brutally honest about our fears about therapy and discuss why shifting our perspective might dramatically improve our quality of life.

How to use what you are learning:

This book is not about forcing you to overhaul every single habit you have. Nor is it about forcing change upon you. It is, however, about exposing you to a perspective and information that you may not have previously considered.

Depressed to Daring

I urge you to lean into what is being presented to you and remain willing to challenge your behavior when necessary. If you can dedicate yourself to being open to the information here, you will change your life.

CHAPTER ONE

BE AGILE, NOT FRAGILE

"Learning agility means to learn, de-learn, and relearn all the times."

— *Pearl Zhu*

When I reflect back on all of the things I've learned along on my path to emotional health, the three things that stand out to me the most are:

1. There seems to be an unspoken rule in both domestic and professional environments that women should never express, discuss, or react to any form of distress.

2. Doing so makes them unfit for any activity where stress can lead to such behavior.

3. As a result, most women neither seek guidance about how to deal with the emotions that inevitably come with stress nor actively surrender to a self-care routine that could help them manage the stress that they aren't supposed to acknowledge in the first place.

A simple internet search reveals that this is especially prevalent amongst high-functioning, educated, success-driven mothers and women, who are in many ways expected to exude professionalism, confidence, and poise when they are on and off the clock.

Furthermore, and speaking from my own experience, if these attributes are problematic behind closed doors, the woman who has unconsciously been trained by society to still do everything in her power to not appear emotional, upset, sad or depressed often complies with the expectation of her outer world, while denying a powerful opportunity for change.

The obvious problem is that by not allowing yourself to experience the natural ebb and flow of emotions, you miss out on valuable opportunities to develop emotional agility and the ability to manage your thoughts and actions while simultaneously observing the emotions associated with challenging external circumstances.

When you habitually suppress negative emotions, you eclipse the possibility of exploring deep-rooted issues that are giving rise to the emotions you are experiencing. Consequently, you are evading the responsibility of better understanding the reason the emotion emerged while cutting yourself off from any other outcome that could result from fully understanding your emotional behavior.

So, what typically happens?

We cling to unhealthy emotional patterns that unconsciously teach us to negate and devalue our gut reaction. If you practice this behavior enough, you train your brain to reach for counterfeit responses that will most likely lead to inauthentic, stoic leadership that doesn't serve you.

By way of example, let's say Woman A aspires to leadership in her company. She's educated, outgoing, and agreeable. She goes above and beyond to support the decisions of her colleagues and build consensus on her team. However, because she is agreeable, she is often overpowered by others who have strong opinions about projects and business decisions. She doesn't talk to anyone about her feelings. She doesn't have a self-care routine. Over time, as she becomes more and more stressed out, beginning to avoid professional situations that trigger negative emotions. As a result, she eventually gets overlooked for advancement opportunities, not because she isn't a good worker, but because she quietly eliminated herself as an option through her inability to deal with whatever feelings were being triggered in her work environment.

To illustrate this another way let's say Woman B is identical to Woman A in every aspect, except, but instead of avoiding professional situations she ends up overcommitted to or overextended by projects because she doesn't want to appear to be a poor sport. Eventually, she gets so overburdened and stressed that she falls behind with projects and ends up overlooked because she appeared to be a poor project manager.

These are two different women dealing with two different work environments, but both are inadvertently using the same logic to make decisions: if I don't want to look bad or feel negative thoughts, I'm going to do whatever is necessary to avoid feeling them. Both end up emotionally and professionally fragile and typically don't realize until it's too late that by avoiding those feelings they weren't keeping up with their ambitions. You see, being in leadership, or being at the helm of any project or company isn't about being agreeable. It's about understanding how to manage your emotions and your actions in a way that is still in alignment with your desired outcome when you aren't. Anything less leaves you fragile and susceptible to self-sabotage.

Emotional agility, on the other hand, offers you an additional skill set by which you can evaluate your feelings, allowing you to observe them without being overwhelmed.

The best way I came to understand the concept was by learning to treat my emotions like clothes. **Some clothes are nicer than others. Some are trendier or more fashionable than** others, and some are of higher quality. Some are more expensive. Some are cheap. Some are simply tried, true, and comfortable. They can be seen, felt, or even admired. Clothes and how you style them can give you a sense of identity, and some make you feel better than others. But at the end of the day, they are all just adornments for your body. You wear them and take them off when you are done with them. And when you outgrow them, you toss them.

In this sense, emotional agility would be wearing what you want to wear, and not being moved to change your outfit because someone said they didn't like it. Furthermore, it would also be the quality of questioning yourself about why you'd want to change just because someone didn't like what you were wearing, and making the decision to change or not based on what you believe to be true about your outfit and how you feel in it.

Being agile instead of fragile helps you identify what your emotional patterns are and how they impact your behavior.

The Anatomy of Agility-Driven Behavior

Agility-driven behavior consists of five key components:
1. Awareness
2. Acceptance
3. Objectivity
4. Ownership
5. Inspired Action

Depressed to Daring

Awareness

The basis of agility is being conscious of your resting place. It is also having awareness about any factors that could impact your emotional health. It's impossible to know when you're experiencing a shift if you don't know where you started. This stage is the starting point for every agility driven-action to follow.

Acceptance

The second stage is acceptance, or being open to whatever emotions arise during your gut reaction. It is showing up for whatever emotions come to the surface and not cutting them off, no matter how they feel.

Objectivity

Stage three is about your ability to observe your emotions and be objective about why you are being triggered into feeling how you feel.

So, let's say you see a picture of your friends having lunch together on social media. Generally speaking, your initial reaction would be to get mad and vow to give all of them the silent treatment until someone explains why you weren't invited. Now, in this case, an objective mindset would enable you:

1. To ask yourself why you are upset. (Does this kind of thing trigger pain from being excluded in high school, for instance?)
2. To consider if this is something that happens all of the time and, if so, why it continues to happen. (Do you break plans

frequently? Do people feel that you would have genuinely enjoyed the occasion?)

And, finally . . .

3. To consider all the possible reasons you could have been excluded. (Is there a possibility that you've just been overlooked? Is it possible that you missed a text, call, or email about the event?)

All before making any vow to take any direct or indirect action.

Ownership

Stage four is owning and accepting the truth behind your triggered emotion. If we continue with the aforementioned example, it would be to accept the truth that, given all of the objective information you have, you may be overreacting based on feelings or experiences that don't have anything to do with that isolated event.

Inspired Action

And lastly, stage five is all about your ability to use the information you've evaluated in a way that is in alignment with your desired outcome. In the scenario above, if your desired outcome is to be invited to the next outing, or on a more consistent basis, then inspired action would be whatever action or behavior is likely to get you an invite. If you were to give everyone the silent treatment, you'd be less likely to get an invite. A more inspired action might be to have a conversation with one or two of the women involved to see how the event came about, and ask to be included next time.

Once you get the hang of it, the applications and possibilities are endless.

Here are a few to consider . . .

Emotional Agility at Home

Integrating the skills of emotional agility at home can help parents nurture resilient children. Additionally, agile parents, through the awareness of their own emotional health, can consciously create a healthy social and emotional environment in which the child can learn. Imagine how beneficial this could be for families who have been stuck in behavioral and emotional cycles.

Emotional Agility in Your Relationships

When used in relationships, romantic or not, emotional agility can help people evaluate the reasons they choose and maintain certain kinds of relationships. While it doesn't guarantee that there won't be fights or disagreements, it can help partners to better understand the motivation behind their behavior and situational reactions.

Emotional Agility in Your Professional Life

We've already explored a few examples of how emotional agility can be beneficial to women in the workplace. But, to expand even further, it arms women with the emotional tools necessary to remain resilient under stress. Not only does it open the door to the upward movement for women in corporate, nonprofit, and political environments, but it allows them to survive more easily in these areas as well.

Depressed to Daring

These are just a few ways emotional agility can be applied in a way that is beneficial for women. What additional ways could you imagine its application in your day-to-day life?

Putting Emotional Agility into Practice

To get started on your emotional agility journey, you must first establish an awareness of your current emotional state. I've created a simple exercise to help you gain awareness of the emotions you feel on a daily basis.

A Starting Place

You will need one piece of paper and two different colored pens. Read all the emotions below and identify the top ten that you feel on a regular basis. From that list of ten, whittle your number down to your most common five emotions (and if emotions you feel are not listed, feel free to add them to the list). Then, without judgment observe whether this makes you pleased, content, or disappointed.

- Abundant
- Annoyed
- Anxious
- Appreciated
- Attractive
- Awed
- Beautiful
- Bored
- Compassionate
- Confident
- Connected
- Discouraged
- Enthusiastic
- Exhausted
- Fearful
- Fulfilled
- Grateful
- Guilty
- Happy
- Hopeful
- Impatient
- Insecure

Depressed to Daring

- Inspired
- Interested
- Intimidated
- Joyful
- Justified
- Love
- Motivated
- Open
- Optimistic
- Passionate
- Passive
- Peaceful
- Productive

- Powerful
- Proud
- Reliable
- Relaxed
- Safe
- Satisfied
- Stressed
- Strong
- Successful
- Trusting
- Uncertain
- Wealthy
- Worthy

What Factors are Impacting You?

Once you have your list of five emotions, draft a paragraph about how or why you believe these emotions are most prevalent in your life. Some things to consider might be your history with . . .

- Anger
- Overcommitment
- Divorce
- Jealousy
- Feelings of Inadequacy
- Abandonment Issues
- Gossip

- Betrayal
- Poverty Mindset
- Generational Curses
- Trauma
- Self-Sacrifice
- Martyrdom
- Narcissistic Partners or Parents

Depressed to Daring

Put it into Action

Lastly, after you've completed the above assignment, get a piece of paper and reflect on the exercise and what you have discovered. Then make this an opportunity to go into the next seven days with more awareness of which feelings arise in particular situations and with whom.

Return to the list after a week, and write down any patterns you identified from your notes Consider ways you may need to alter your behavior in situations where you were disappointed with the outcomes.

IN CASE NO ONE HAS TOLD YOU:

You deserve to live and work in environments that allow you to show up and be present for the range of emotions you feel. You have the power to observe your behavior and change your circumstances by being agile.

CHAPTER TWO

TRANSFORM YOUR TRANSACTIONS

"Change starts in your thoughts."

— Anonymous

In the weeks that followed my election loss, I couldn't stop thinking about all of the things that had gone wrong. I focused on the details of my defeat trying to figure out what I could have done to change the outcome. I constantly replayed each piece of advice I hadn't followed. I replayed conversations from friends and strangers over and over until a point of exhaustion, carefully combing each encounter for clues regarding what might have been overlooked, ignored, or even misunderstood.

I felt incredibly guilty for not doing a better job of preparing my family for the emotional and financial stress of campaigning. I felt ripped apart by the opinions of complete strangers, and there were many days when I wrestled with the sharp pain of inadequacy, disappointed in myself for letting down the young women that I had mentored and supported in the years prior. I spent minutes, hours, days, and weeks, completely consumed by reruns of situations that I'd had no control over.

In my quest to understand, I had unknowingly deepened my habit of negative self-talk, which only resulted in me feeling more and more isolated and depressed.

Although there were people who offered support when I went out into the community and others who sent words of encouragement, I repeatedly told myself that there was no coming back from the shame of such a public loss. It was like I forfeited any right to happiness and wanted to remind myself that my defeated position was earned, because if what people felt wasn't true, then I wouldn't have ended up with the outcome that had come about. Perhaps my ego had been too large, and I just wasn't seeing myself correctly.

Depressed to Daring

Even though there were no physical wounds, and I was free to resume my life with my kids and go about my day-to-day activities, I resolved to imprison myself in my mind for a little longer, unofficially sentencing myself to a handful of negative thoughts each day. I felt it would have been a betrayal to be happy, as though I hadn't learned my lessons or acknowledged where I had messed up or made errors.

I was deeply and unhealthily dedicated to my negative thought patterns. In fact, any day when I got dangerously close to contentment, I would quickly eclipse my attention to it, and isolate myself until I returned to the gloomy shadow of my worst thoughts.

When friends called or texted, I would retell the story of how bad it was. I would confess my sins and apologize profusely so that they would have proof that I was still in debt to my embarrassment.

When they stopped calling, I started to wonder if my self-imposed sentence should be over. I wondered if enough time had passed for me to reasonably return to society, somehow absolved through my absence from the limelight.

Roughly six weeks after the loss, I started to venture out, keeping my interactions brief but authentic. I started to return calls and respond to messages on Facebook. I started to enjoy the little things again, like the hum of the stove fan after I made dinner, or the way my youngest son would situate himself next to me on the couch when he was ready for a nap, or the way the sheets felt on the coldest, foggiest mornings in Pacifica, right before I had to get out of bed to get the kids ready for school.

As I started to feel better, I slowly returned to the activities I loved.

I even made it to the local high school to run around the track a few times. Being there, doing warm-up drills in the dewy moist air with Elton John's "Still Standing," blaring in my ear, seemed to be the perfect remedy to the sadness I'd been experiencing.

And it worked for a while. Exercising definitely alleviated the barrage of negative self-talk, and gave me something to focus my energy on other than defeat.

It was working so well, and my mood had improved so much, that I actually felt I was healing simply by working out. Until one day, in the middle of a two hundred-meter sprint, when a notification sound went off in my headphones. Since I was expecting an email from a colleague, I slowed my pace for a few strides to check the preview message.

It wasn't from my anticipated sender but from another friend.

The preview line read "I thought you would want to see this."

Now, I know I should have ignored the message or deleted it, especially because I was doing so well, but I'm human, and my curiosity got the best of me and proceeded to open and read the message.

I wish I hadn't.

I ended my workout and headed back up the street to my home.

I walked in, took a shower, grabbed a fistful of lunchmeat from the fridge, and hopped into bed. Within a matter of minutes, I was back in my room, nestled in bed, cycling the negative self-talk that I swore I'd never examine again.

"It makes no sense to worry about things you have no control over because there's nothing you can do about them, and why worry about things you do control? The activity of worrying keeps you immobilized."
— Wayne Dyer

Thoughts are Emotional Transactions

Whether or not you've suffered a public loss, chances are that you have experienced some level of sorrow, guilt, shame, embarrassment, humiliation, or deep heartbreak. And, while lingering feelings associated with whatever you've been through is completely normal, overthinking your experience isn't. Aside from the fact that negative self-talk can do massive damage to your mental state, and even heighten your stress and anxiety level, it is also an incredibly difficult habit to break. Constantly dwelling on your pain is a self-destructive behavior that will predictably send you further into depression if you allow it.

It is one thing to endure the weight of a sad or traumatic experience; it is another to forfeit your identity to that sadness. Some people become so loyal to their loss that they lose weeks, if not months on end, searching for validation from their tears.

I have done this. I have looked for my self-worth amongst the rubble, and I assure you what you are looking for isn't there. You will have to recreate it, and no one can do that for you. It must be a personal choice.

I believe that every thought you have creates a tiny cord between the mind and the spirit, and the quality of those thoughts determines your emotional and mental strength. The higher the quality of thought, the thicker the cord; the poorer the quality, the weaker the cord.

Therefore, if you are focused on high-quality thoughts, you can strengthen the connection between your mind and spirit. The problem is that when you are facing something difficult, you focus on low-quality thoughts, and although those cords are weaker, if you dwell on them enough, they can collectively become stronger than the few high-quality thoughts that protect the foundation of your mental strength. The positive side to this is that If you are conscious about your thoughts, you can strengthen your mind and spirit, even when you aren't living in the best circumstances. You always have the potential to dramatically improve your mind, in the same way, that you can completely obliterate every shred of self-esteem you have with negative thinking. It's what you focus on that determines the outcome.

If your mind is your most sacred place, then anything that you allow through its doors or allow to dwell within its walls will contribute to who you are—be that the weakest or the most empowered, esteemed version of yourself.

Quality Over Quantity

In the last chapter, we discussed how beneficial emotional agility can be when it comes to giving yourself space to objectively evaluate your emotions. Doing so, one can take inspired action that leads to less ego-driven decisions.

In this chapter I submit to you another consideration: while it is beneficial to observe our emotions to develop a sense of resilience and grit, it is equally as important to be conscious about the emotions you choose to evaluate.

Experts estimate that the mind has between sixty and eighty thousand thoughts per day. This works out to an average of twenty-five hundred thoughts per hour!

I don't know about you, but I'm a busy mom, my calendar is comfortably full, and even when I have downtime, it is minimal. So, it would be an arduous, stress-inducing task, to evaluate each of these thoughts just to become agile.

Instead, I've learned that in order to maintain my commitment to developing agility, I must determine which thoughts deserve my attention, and thus my emotional investment. I call it "Spend. Give. Save."

Use "Spend. Give. Save." Decide What to Focus on

"Spend. Give. Save" is a method I've used to organize my time for years. I've more recently adapted it to organize my emotional attention. This method is my personal commitment to prioritizing my attention and focusing on things that are the most important to me. Through this commitment:

1. I spend my emotional attention on people and things that make me feel my best.
2. I give my emotional attention to things that I value.
3. And I save a portion of my emotional attention for myself, and the boundaries around my personal truth.

Within the framework of emotional agility development, you would use "Spend. Give. Save" to determine which emotions should be prioritized for evaluation. You would leverage your attention to your certain emotions like currency. You would only invest that currency on the things that would yield a solid return.

If you can strike a balance with the things you should focus on and the emotional behavior you want to alter, you can improve your chances of success when it comes to creating a sense of emotional balance within yourself. To achieve such a balance, you have to be willing to critically examine your reasons and beliefs about the things you can and cannot control. When it comes to your home and work life there are a lot of things that you can witness or experience, but still not control. For example:

- You can give your child the life you never had as a child, but it wouldn't mean that they would value it the same way you do.

Depressed to Daring

- You can be qualified for your dream job, and apply, but still not be called back for an interview.
- You can be the most successful, eligible bachelorette in your local community but still not be asked on a date.
- You can attempt to manipulate your kids to go to a certain school or choose a certain major, but you can't guarantee they will do so, or follow through with the level of excitement that you're expecting.
- You can exercise every day to alleviate stress, but you can't avoid dealing with your behavioral health.

Putting "Spend. Give. Save" into Practice

To determine the thoughts and the emotions that deserve your investment, you must recognize the things you find valuable. Below is an exercise that helps you gain clarity about the things that should be high on your emotional attention list.

Instructions

I want you to create three different lists with five bullets under each title, Spend, Give, and Save. Then I want you to assign five things you want to spend your emotional attention on, five things you want to give your emotional attention to, and five things that represent your personal truth, that you want to Save or spare for yourself.

Here is an example of how to set this up.

Spend
*
*

*
*
*

Give
*
*
*
*
*

Save
*
*
*
*
*

Leverage Your Attention Strategically

Once you have all fifteen spaces filled, I want you to write a letter to yourself describing how you will prioritize and protect each of those areas of your attention over the next thirty days. In this letter, I also want you to consider which external factors are beyond your control. Also, predict how you might react if the things you decide are priorities for you don't turn out to be priorities for others. So, for example, you can state that you want to devote your emotional attention to your aunt Liz, but you have no control over whether or not she wants to use her time to focus on you at this point in her life. Being consciously aware of these factors will help you discern whether or not attention needs to be given to something, how or why your attention may not be reciprocated, and where to focus in situations that are largely beyond your control.

For me, I found that my anxiety would be heightened when I focused on things that I couldn't control, so I made a goal to shift my thoughts away negative thinking if I found myself dwelling on a matter for more than two days in a row. Here's what happened:

- **My Relationships Improved**

    When I learned to stop making people feel bad about me, my circumstances, or things I was personally going through, my relationships deepened. By giving up control over their perception, I learned to go with the flow, and the people who naturally aligned with my life's path found me. It also made it easier to ask for help when I needed help. I felt more at ease with the people who were around me because I knew their presence in my life was genuine and that I hadn't done or said anything to get them to stay.

- **New Doors Opened**

    As I learned to shift my mind away from negative thought patterns, I opened my time up to experiences that I would have never considered. In the past, I would avoid situations that made me feel uneasy or anxious, but when I stopped focusing on those things, I found myself going to places I'd never heard of, with people I'd never met.

- **I Wrote a New Story**

    The most exciting thing about shifting away from negative thoughts and your past failures or defeats is that you'll eventually meet people who don't know a thing about you or your past. These people are gifts from the universe. They come to give you a chance to tell a new story about yourself.

Transforming How You Think

If you focus on what's wrong with your circumstances, you are going to find more of what's wrong with them. If you do this for extended periods of time, you'll lose valuable opportunities to address issues. Transforming your thoughts is a matter of shifting your perception away from the belief that you have control over the outcome to be happy. It also means understanding that you deserve to be happy and content in spite of whatever lead up to the outcome. You cannot turn back time. You cannot undo your past. You can also use it as wisdom and move your life forward. A daring woman who can avoid dwelling on the past and things beyond her control understands:

- That her self-worth isn't tied to any particular outcome.
- Negative thoughts don't help her move towards balance in her emotional life.
- Opinions aren't facts, and operating as though they are eclipses opportunities to grow and thrive in her home and in business.

IN CASE NO ONE HAS TOLD YOU

You are your most powerful investor. The way you spend your attention determines what you can afford in one week, one month, or one year from now. Do not drain your account and go into emotional bankruptcy over thoughts that are not equally invested in you.

CHAPTER THREE

MIND YOUR GAP

"Emotion triggers action, good or otherwise."

— *Pieter BF Swart*

When I was married, I used to have these fall-out, eye-for-an-eye, winner-take-all arguments with my spouse.

Sometimes we would argue over really big things, like how we'd want to approach socializing the kids, what kind of snacks the kids should be allowed to have, over schooling, or which insurance company had the most competitive rates. And in other instances, we'd argue over small things like who'd left the milk out, why the kids were eating macaroni and cheese for the third day in a row, or if I really needed to go to Target to get construction paper at 10:45 pm (my answer was yes, by the way). But in most instances, in our quest to prove our reasoning or logic for our position, all rationality went out the window the moment one of us was triggered.

Sound familiar?

Your brain is one of your most powerful organs. It controls all functions of your body. It controls your thoughts, memories, and speech patterns. It also protects you by rationalizing your behavior. When something happens, you react, and then your brain creates a reason for your reaction, seemingly justifying your behavior— even if that reason isn't factually sound.

Let's say, you get upset with your spouse because you can't find your keys. You go on a tirade and blame your spouse for being inconsiderate and making you late. You also completely ignore any logical reason why you could be reacting in this manner or what your part in the problem was. From the outside looking in, it's obvious that you neglected to organize your belongings, including the car keys, the night before, but why was that so hard to see in the moment? It's because your brain kicked in and helped you rationalize your actions that day based on some random memory from 2003 when your sister borrowed your car, returned it with an empty tank, and you were forced to stop for gas on the way to an interview for your dream job. Then, as the result of stopping for gas, you ended up in traffic and late for the most important day of your life. Despite the fact that you got the job, you subconsciously carried the concern that you were perceived as inconsiderate or behind the ball by the company. Whether you knew it or not, you vowed to never feel that feeling of defeat ever again, and you also decided that anyone who was a hindrance to your ability to be perceived as successful should take the blame.

Like it or not, while we are very much able to able to imagine our dream life, leap entire buildings in Jimmy Choo shoes, and scale the towers of success in fabulous dresses from Rent the Runway, we can't outrun the hardwiring of our DNA and pretend that we aren't sometimes the root cause of some of our greatest disappointments.

The biggest shock to my system during my post-divorce therapy session was learning and accepting the fact that my behavioral habits were culprits in the unweaving of my relationship. Like, seriously, how could I be this dynamic powerhouse of a woman in my professional life but fall victim to emotional patterns in my home life? Well, it was because I was unconsciously allowing my brain to rationalize my behavior by not addressing feelings that were emotionally triggering me. I was not introducing any data that would have suggested that the beliefs, thoughts, and actions I was taking, were incorrect.

Your Beliefs are Just Thoughts You Keep Thinking

Your beliefs, *not to be confused with your faith or religious preferences*, are the main characters in the story you have created about your existence.

Consciously or not, you have adopted a network of beliefs from your family, your upbringing, your culture, the media, pop-culture, education, and personal experiences. Once you decided that something was true and it became a part of your story, the foundations for a habit of thoughts were formed, keeping elements of your story neatly tucked away. When you repeatedly enforced those thoughts through your attention to them, you established your belief system, and that system has set the tone for every action you have taken ever since.

By extension, if you hold the belief that you are poor, unattractive, or not good at a particular task, your thoughts create a reality that brings more evidence to support that belief system. If you believe that you are not good enough for certain people, the world then delivers evidence of such, through events that will reinforce those core beliefs.

Mind Your Gap

When you are triggered by something, it's your brain's way of showing you that something in your environment does not line up with the belief or the story you have formed about yourself. The thing, the emotion, the automatic emotional response, that exists in the gap between your beliefs and your thoughts is where triggers live. The information hidden in those gaps isn't accounted for in our belief system. So, if we are going to be honest about our behavior and how it helps or hinders us in domestic and professional environments, then we have to learn how to mind our gap.

As women, minding our gap means being vigilant about the thoughts we allow ourselves to give attention to. We might not have control over every thought that crosses our minds, but we do have control over the ones that fuel our beliefs about our value, our worth, and our own self-perception.

What are Emotional Triggers?

Emotional triggers are those incredibly sensitive and over-reactive places deep inside you that become activated when the behavior or comments of someone else, or just an outside event or circumstance, do not line up with your emotional belief system. Some people respond to triggers by lashing out and taking extreme actions, while others simply withdraw or cope through the use of drugs or alcohol.

In most cases, one feels a sense of regret or anger after they have coped or reacted in a way that was negative. For example, let's say you go out for drinks with a couple of friends. You struggle to find something to wear because your weight has been fluctuating and most of your clothes are too tight. Nonetheless, you choose something for yourself that you find to be appealing or flattering, only to have one of your friends tell you that you look like you're trying too hard to get attention because of how you are dressed. Instead of revealing to your friend that you've been experiencing health issues that have caused fluctuations in your appearance or that you found her comment to be rude, you say some nasty words and leave the restaurant. In this situation, the triggers would be your beliefs about bodyweight and the kind of attire you feel would be appropriate for the event, your relationship with the friend you made the comment, your overreaction, and lastly, your ability to say *no* to situations that you know will have a negative impact on your mental health.

> "When things are challenging, remember you are not the feelings and emotions. They are just a reaction to the situation, so accept them and try to find the root source and ease that pain - The core essence of you is a beautiful, unique, authentic spirit and you are worth of everything in life."
> — Nanette Mathews

Get Real

I'm going to let you in on a little secret: no matter how educated you are, or how successful, there are things about yourself that need some attention. *Getting Real* means you start noticing when you are set off by the actions of others. It means doing a self-check when something is upsetting and you're tempted to respond in a certain way. You are the weaver of your own dreams and the achiever of your own ambitions, but you are also the person responsible for every version of yourself while you in pursuit of your goal.

Before we can get real about our own habits, we have to allow ourselves to identify them. Start listening to your response when someone you don't particularly care for asks for help on a project, and then observe how you respond when another colleague asks you to do something. Be willing to acknowledge whether or not the energy you are giving off is making it easier or harder to work with certain people—or for them to want to work with you. We tend to write people off the minute they do something we don't like and cast them into a category that determines how we should treat them from that day forward.

I used to be in this professional organization several years ago. It was a service organization that was full of a lot of high-performing, kick-ass, I-eat-nails-for-breakfast, go-getter women. I loved it, and I loved being connected to so many amazing, accomplished people. The problem I often ran into was that I'd always reach an impasse with other women who had personalities that were just as strong as my own, or who were just as accomplished as me. So, if we were working on a project and I wanted things to go a certain way, I'd employ certain behaviors to try to establish dominance over the other person. The minute they did something I didn't like, I'd do my email response-time flex habit where I would wait days to respond to emails because I didn't want to appear to be available to them. And when I did respond, I'd offer unsolicited advice on whatever project we were working on, just to prove that I was just as useful to the team, if not more so.

The issue with doing this was over time I started to realize I wasn't extended opportunities to collaborate as frequently, and when I was, the timelines would be so tight that I'd almost have to defer to the other collaborators. Has this happened to you? Have you found yourself in a professional situation when you responded to people in a certain way so you appeared to be of value?

In hindsight, by allowing my feelings of inadequacy and powerlessness to trigger me when I was around other people who were equally or sometimes more experienced than me, I cut myself out of opportunities to contribute.

> "Triggers are like little psychic explosions that crash through avoidance and bring the dissociated, avoided trauma suddenly, unexpectedly, back into consciousness."
>
> — Carolyn Spring

Put it into Practice. Track Your Triggers

If you want to Get Real about your patterns, grab a piece of paper and make a list of the common behaviors you exhibit in different environments (i.e. work, school, volunteer committees, etc.). If you want to take it a step further, also consider how you behave around people from another culture or another race or how you act when you are working with established men. Make note of:

How frequently you get upset . . .

What you do when you feel outranked . . .

How you behave if you are repeatedly overlooked or not considered . . .

Whether or not you make friends with people you perceive to be a threat to you . . .

What you do when you feel unsupported by your boss. . .

Depressed to Daring

How you cope . . .

How often you indulge in wine or alcohol after a hard day . . .

How frequently you feel confident in those environments . . .

Whether or not you feel valued and why . . .

    Another way to identify your triggers is to look at the areas of your life that aren't thriving. If you're constantly angry, anxious, or depressed, you might be caught in a vicious cycle of triggering behavior that reinforces whatever belief system you have surrounded yourself with. Your behavior subconsciously creates patterns in your life that you are used to navigating, so if you are noticing that a lot of the stories you are telling yourself or the people around you about your circumstances start or end the same way, perhaps it's because your behavior from experience-to-experience is the same as well. If it is, this could indicate areas of your life that need to be developed so you can overcome the barriers to up-leveling in your life or career.

    If you don't have a weekly practice of journaling, then this is your perfect opportunity to start one. Writing your realizations down is a great way to track your triggers and get a visual picture of the areas of your life that need some work.

    It's easy to believe the illusion that when we feel justified or righteous in our behavior that there won't be any real consequences to our actions, but there are always consequences. The Law of Cause and Effect states that success in any field of endeavor is a direct result of specific causes and actions and that success in any field of endeavor is an indirect result of specific causes and actions. This means that if you repeatedly behave in a certain way, like with certain triggers, for example, there will be a predictable outcome. It doesn't matter if there is a reason or justification in the mix. It simply means the trajectory of your career or opportunities will be determined by your behavior.

On the flip side, it also means that if you make the right decisions and take the right actions, you will undoubtedly achieve the success you envision for your life. Being emotionally agile requires you to deal with issues head-on, as opposed to avoiding them, but success in this feat, especially when it comes to triggers, is knowing what your triggers are, what causes them, and how you react to them, so you can change the outcome of predictable events.

IN CASE NO ONE HAS TOLD YOU

You may not always be able to control the people or the circumstances that trigger your emotions, but through mindfulness and awareness to your responses, you can create an anchor that keeps you present and in a position to change the patterns. Calm the mind, and listen to your inner voice.

CHAPTER FOUR

SURRENDER TO SELF-CARE

"Nourishing yourself in a way that helps you blossom in the direction you want to go is attainable, and you are worth the effort."

— Deborah Day

When I was in my early twenties, I wanted nothing more than to be a reporter. I ate, drank, and slept news. I had dreams of being the next Katie Couric or Oprah. At the time, I was living in Los Angeles, and I was surrounded by so many people who had careers in front of the camera that it seemed inevitable that I, too, would make the jump to becoming a successful reporter.

And it was. A few years after undergrad I was able to land my first, full-time gig as a weather anchor and reporter for a local news station. I was married, with a two-year-old, living out my childhood dreams in front of an audience of hundreds of thousands of people. I had a good group of friends who, not surprisingly, were all also reporters and anchors at the local station, and my life was tracking along, just the way I had always planned it. Except for two things. In my quest to obtain the life of my dreams, I was so consumed with "looking the part," that I wasn't taking good care of myself, and I wasn't paying attention to the little distress signals my body was giving me. Distress signals like moodiness, anxiety, stomach knots, insomnia, constant cramping, panic attacks, and migraines had become a part of my daily norm.

On some days I was up as early as 3 a.m. so I could get to the station before my newscast. I would work until 1 or 2 p.m., and then I went home and tried to live a mostly normal life with my toddler and husband. Despite the early mornings, I still came home and cooked, cleaned, and spent time with my family. Some nights I'd stay up to watch the later broadcasts so I would know how my story did, or see what to expect in the morning. Although I was slowly burning the candle on both ends, I didn't see any issue with my habits. At twenty-five, I figured that it was just something I would have to get used to

Depressed to Daring

until I established a name for myself, and that it would eventually go away as long as I held my position on the news team and continued to work hard.

How wrong I was.

One night, I went to sleep as usual. Although I wasn't feeling well earlier in the day, I figured a couple of Tylenol would do the trick and that by morning I'd be good to go. Except, at roughly 5 a.m., I had the most bizarre dream. In the dream I was awake and getting ready to go to work, but while I was getting ready, I experienced terrible cramps. In my dream state, I felt pain that was near the equivalent of birth contractions. While I was experiencing this in my dream, I turned to my husband in bed and told him that I needed to go to the hospital. When he didn't wake up, I got worried. I then realized that I wasn't awake, and that I was actually stuck in a dream within a dream. Upon realizing this, I made a conscious decision to force myself to wake up, thinking that the pain would go away once the dream was over. So, I forced myself awake, and lay in bed still for a moment. And a moment was all it took for me to realize that the paid wasn't fake. In fact, it was ten times worse, now that I was awake. I shook my husband, and told him I needed to go to the hospital, which was a thirty-minute drive from our home in Soledad to Salinas. Within fifteen minutes, we were are all dressed and in the car. As we drove, I tried to review everything I had eaten in the last week. My initial presumption was that perhaps I had a case of food poisoning.

But I was wrong. After about an hour of testing at the hospital, the doctor came out and informed me that I my appendix was rupturing and that I needed to have emergency surgery. He told me that I wouldn't be able to carry anything heavy for at least six weeks after the surgery—not even my daughter—and that I wouldn't be able to go back to work until they felt I had healed properly.

In what felt like the longest moment of my life, everything changed. My time at the station would come to an abrupt end, and due to my inattention to my stress level, and factors contributing to it, there was nothing I could do but let go.

Self-Care 101

Self-care is any behavior or activity that you consciously apply to enhance, protect, or restore your mental, emotional, or physical health. With respect to emotional agility, self-care is the mechanism you would leverage to reflect on and release the feelings, emotions, or thoughts that do not align with your highest good. So, for example, if you are practicing emotional agility with a friend, colleague or work situation, and although you are leaning into the uncomfortable feelings that come with your new outlook, you still have very valid feelings and emotions related to the way things have unfolded. Self-care, then, would be your conscious decision to devote some time to release those feelings. Self-care puts you back on track with your truth, and it allows you to hold boundaries around the parts of you that need to be protected. It anchors you, and it will help you maintain your emotional groundedness, no matter the circumstances.

Speaking only for myself, it seems like the self-care movement wasn't trendy until recent years. I remember a time, before this cultural shift to self-love and self-care, when it would have been frowned upon for anyone, especially women, to set boundaries around their mental health and overall wellbeing. For many of us, there has always been this lie that was perpetuated in most workplaces that we have to endure to be respected. We've been conditioned to believe that being able to shoulder any and all kinds of abuse, strain, or stress in all areas of our lives somehow makes us stronger than our counterparts, or even other women. But if there's anything I've learned from having an emergency surgery, and having my life dramatically re-routed because I didn't listen to my body, is that this belief that you will feel more worthy, be more valued, or find esteem by ignoring the practice of balance, mindfulness, and self-care, is an illusion. Feeding into it bolsters this belief that your health is less important than the accolades, acknowledgement, or professional respect that might come at the expense of your health. This thinking is misguided, and is a silent killer to women and their mental health everywhere.

Workaholism is not a virtue. Overworking yourself and taking on the stress and exhaustion that comes with constant strain makes you less productive, and it can leave you emotionally depleted. Being emotionally agile requires you to be mindful of your thoughts, actions, and behaviors. It also requires that you set and leverage boundaries around your personal limits so you can maintain balance.

Boundaries, Boundaries, Boundaries

Creating and sustaining boundaries is a skill. But for some women, especially those struggling with codependent behavior, boundary-building is a newer concept and one that proves to be challenging. Knowing when to draw the line and knowing what your limits are the create the foundation of self-care. Healthy boundaries allow us to build a line between ourselves and the outside world. In addition to our professional life, the outside world can also include relationships with friends and family, commitments, beliefs, negative thoughts, naysayers, narcissists and your past mistakes. On an emotional level, setting boundaries helps us separate our feelings, needs, beliefs, and our personal truth from others. One example of this is your ability to state your truth and be grounded enough to not shoulder any blame for how others receive it.

Could you imagine a country without borders, or a freeway without lanes freeway? People would roam about or drive where they saw fit. Boundaries provide a sense of structure in our lives, and when we actively set them, on our own terms, we reclaim the space we hold as women in the world. When we forfeit this skill, and allow others and their will to change the structure of our lives, we unknowingly give our power away—often to things and people who do not honor our authentic truth.

So, how do you set boundaries?

1. **Get Clear.**

   Be honest about your limits, and know where you stand. Make a list, and determine where your emotional, mental, and spiritual boundaries lie. If there are things about your emotional or mental wellbeing that are non-negotiable, note them. Know what you can and cannot tolerate. Know who or what triggers, depletes, or ungrounds you. The difference between contentment and stress, confidence and a mental fog, is where the boundaries exist. Get clear on what that space feels like to you.

2. **Get Real About Your Emotions.**

    When you gain clarity around the feelings that are triggered in certain situations, or when you don't live up to the expectations of others, you can and will make better decisions about the things that deserve more or less of your attention.

3. **Show Up For Yourself!**

    It's wonderful to have boundaries, but they don't mean anything until you communicate with other people when they intrude in your emotional space. Be willing to give people the opportunity to love and respect you the way you want to be honored. Wallowing in pity, negative self-talk, shame and guilt only creates cycles of self-fulfilling prophecies about your negative beliefs. If someone crosses a line, it is your responsibility to tell them. Let them know what your expectations are.

4. **Go Back to Go Forward.**

    Consider how your childhood and formative experiences have influenced your current relationships. Ask yourself if you self-identify as the "good child," the caretaker, the know-it-all, or the black sheep. Be critical of your current relationships and look for ways you might be recreating the dynamic that played out in your home life, and how it's manifesting in your current reality.

What do boundaries look like?

Depressed to Daring

Self-care boundaries in the workplace look like:

- Telling your boss you can't take on additional projects.
- Not working when you aren't being compensated for it.
- Getting enough sleep during the week to make good decisions and function properly.
- Accepting jobs that offer perks for mental health.
- Saying no to colleagues who make you feel like your effort isn't good enough.
- Sticking to a work cut-off time and not picking up your laptop because you're bored.
- Actually, using your vacation days throughout the year to take a break, even if it is only a staycation.
- Having friends who are in different industries and fields so you have an outlet, and friends who can offer a different perspective.
- Saying no to workplace relationships.
- Not using your money to fund company projects or expenses.
- Carving out time for your kids' activities, even if they fall in the middle of the day, and making arrangements for them with your job in advance.
- Eating a balanced diet.
- Asking for a raise if you have the data and analytics to back up your request.
- Saying no to events or invitations that will not benefit your career.
- Communicating to your colleagues or boss when you feel someone is abusing their power.
- Taking an actual lunch and understanding the break's rules. (If you are allowed to leave the office, then go for a walk. If you have a flexible lunch, use it to get a midday workout in.)

- Saying no to excessive work that was not in your job description.
- Asking for a work performance review, so that you can get clear on what you need to work on.
- Using your right to file formal complaints against others in the workplace if they have crossed the line, violated a law, or have otherwise acted in a way that makes you feel uncomfortable.
- Wearing your hair in a way that makes you feel comfortable.
- Wearing or styling clothes that make you feel confident, daring, and exciting.

I want to be clear that all companies are not openly progressive when it comes to work life balance, but that doesn't mean you should shy away from getting clarity around what you can and cannot do. **Small doses of stress are completely normal and give us the nudge to work harder to meet deadlines, or knock out problems before they become bigger problems, but they alone should not be the drivers of discomfort that keep us in a mental gridlock with anxiety, fear, and depressing thoughts.** Being smart about your self-care routines helps you to manage your emotions and feelings in a way that is balanced and well thought out.

Self-care boundaries in your friendships and relationships look like:

- Cutting people who are negative or who always gossip from your life.
- Opting to stay at home or make other plans instead of being around people who make you feel inadequate.
- Cutting your friends off financially if you are covering their expenses and they have not paid you back.

Depressed to Daring

- Ending a relationship because you've outgrown someone.
- Not sharing every detail about your life if you haven't yet figured out your personal truth.
- Not sharing your deepest, darkest problems with people who aren't likely to help.
- Refusing to pay for people who don't make as much money as you.
- Not feeling guilty or ashamed for living a lifestyle that is more affluent than that of friends in your circle.
- Not acting as a reference for people who you do not fully trust.
- Refusing to give up your beliefs, even if they are different from those of your friends.
- Cutting off relationships that do not serve your highest good.

Some might argue that your friendships and relationships should offer a meaningful place for you to be yourself, offer your truth, and to bare it all. But I would argue otherwise. Yes, friendships and relationships can be a construct for respect and enjoyment, but if we're being honest, all relationships and friendships are NOT created equally. And they don't need to be. When we try to force others to follow a narrow set of rules, we set ourselves up for pain, betrayal, and heartache. Everyone doesn't have the maturity or life experience to understand what we've experienced. Self-care is just as much about setting boundaries as it is discernment. Being emotionally agile is about leveraging that inner knowledge of what is and isn't helpful to your belief system, and being critical and selective about the thoughts you allow to enter your psyche.

Depressed to Daring

Self-care boundaries with family look like:

- Cutting your adult child off financially because they are able to earn a living for themselves.
- Taking time for yourself once a week.
- Spending your money on the things you want.
- Asking your spouse or your kids to chip in around the house.
- Staying away from uncomfortable or unsatisfying family gatherings.
- Not paying for unexpected expenses like hospital bills, funerals, child care costs, rent, groceries or other necessities for a relative that you do not have a trusting, loving, and deep tie with.
- Moving away from your family to blaze your own path.
- Choosing a major that excites you, even if your family doesn't agree.
- Not going to college if it's not right for you.
- Not marrying a certain type of person if you don't see them making you happy.
- Being out and being proud about being out! Don't apologize for who you are!
- Blocking relatives that send you reverse compliments, or who only come around to see what you're not doing.
- Not explaining why you aren't in a relationship any longer.
- Not explaining your divorce.
- Not tolerating relatives that berate you when they are drunk or otherwise intoxicated.

    I love going to Thanksgiving dinner and being ripped to shreds because I changed my major, lost my job, and ended a relationship . . . said NO woman ever. So, why do we do it? Why do we put ourselves in situations with people we know are bad for our mental health? Is it an obligation? Is it because deep down we want to feel loved? Or is it because we are so used to the dysfunction that we don't even realize how it's contributing to our poor mental health? I say all of the above. I also say it's normal to wrestle with those feelings, until people are crossing your boundaries, and your mental health is suffering because you're subjecting yourself to people who are not doing the emotional work to address the way they interact with you or others.

"When you are compassionate with yourself, you trust in your soul, which you let guide your life.

— John O'Donohue

Life is such a precious gift. Why waste it doing things that rob you of your confidence? I know we all have huge responsibilities in our work and home lives, and I know it is tempting to attend one dinner, take one more call, or answer one more email, but that interaction can be the thing that sends you over the edge. And while you cannot control each experience that is coming at you, you can control whether-or-not you willingly subject yourself to it.

The trick is to leverage self-care so frequently and effortlessly that you never get to a state of depletion. For me, depletion is like no man's land. It is a place of Limbo. If you've ever seen the movie *Inception*, then you know Limbo is a dimension that allows the dreamer's deepest desires to manifest, but it also unwittingly traps them in a world where they lose their awareness. In other words, no sense of boundaries, and a lack of self-care practices can and will lead to emotional bankruptcy. And in that place of deficiency, you'll do and take almost anything, not realizing that you are feeding a false sense of security.

"With every act of self-care your authentic self gets stronger, and the critical, fearful mind gets weaker. Every act of self-care is a powerful declaration: I am on my side, I am on my side, each day I am more and more on my own side."

— Susan Weiss Berry

Get Radical about Self-Care

There comes a time in every woman's life when she must decide if she's in or out. She must decide if she wants to live the life she's always imagined for herself or if she wants to settle for the status quo. Living the life you've always pictured for yourself means you are willing to do whatever it takes to protect, enhance, or restore your emotional and mental health. It means you are willing to create a self-care plan, stick to it, and set boundaries between yourself and the things that do not serve you. Settling for the status quo means you are willing to continue getting beat up by the negative or detrimental thoughts, opinions, and circumstances that surround you.

Getting radical about who you are in this world, your voice, and what you bring to the table will be one of the most transformative experiences you ever undergo. But I assure you, with clarity and proper planning, you can become the daring, confident, emotionally grounded woman I believe you are, and you'll be so self-assured by your dedication to yourself by doing so, you'll learn to surf the waves of uncertainty with ease.

A woman who believes in radical self-care can:

- Slay the dragons of self-doubt in five-inch heels after a four-hour board meeting.
- Take the boulders of opinion, form them into bricks with her hands, and build the foundation of a career that empowers her.
- Hurdle mountains of anxiety in single bounds.
- Shred feelings of inadequacy with razor sharp confidence in her ability to bounce back after defeat.
- Stretch the limits of space and time by continuously investing in herself, even when she stumbles, and is forced to start again.
- Tackle the thieves of joy with self-belief in her ability to transform in such a way that makes her proud.

Surrendering to this process of putting yourself first, you must lay the foundation for your mental strength. Emotional agility asks us to show up for the fight, be discerning about our thoughts, and to be confident and brave enough to stand by our truths, *but self-care* gives us the inner strength to keep going, and to be in a position of groundedness so we can make decisions that always serve our highest good.

So how do you get radical?

1. **Commit to a Plan.**

    Think about a time frame you can schedule for yourself each week to spend alone with your thoughts. Schedule that time on your calendar, and let your friends and family know that is untouchable.

2. **Try to Do It Without Alcohol.**

   Gasp! Hold your pearls ladies. Yep, that's right. I said it. I want you to try to commit to a self-care plan that doesn't include indulgence. The opposite of the stress isn't over-excitement, or exhilaration; It's contentment. And putting a depressant like alcohol, or any other substance into your body during times of reflection, might disrupt your ability to critically evaluate how you are feeling and why.

3. **Mix It Up**

   I love the Ritz-Carlton. I love silk robes and fuzzy slippers. But there are so many other ways to relax or enjoy time alone. If you want radical results, you have to take radical action. Below are several ideas you should consider adding into your self-care plan.

   - Take a sabbatical. Believe it or not, there are people that actually do this, and they experience a tremendous amount of growth by doing so. Taking one day off of work isn't going to seriously address months of trauma from your boss or co-workers. Book that ticket girl! The world is waiting.

   - Get in a hot air balloon. Hot balloons are super fun. They are beautiful, colorful, and best of all, there's probably no Wi-Fi up there, so at the very least you'll get some uninterrupted time.

   - Create a burn book, and then actually burn it. Unless you're living under a rock, there's a chance you've heard of the idea of a burn book from the movie

"Mean Girls." In the movie they used the book to talk about their classmates, but in the self-care movement of 2020 we have better things to do—like draft letters to people who have really hurt us in the past. On the flip side, you can also use it to write notes and letters to people you feel that you may have wronged or otherwise hurt through your actions and your words. After you fill all of the pages with your words, you can literally burn it, in a firepit for example, to symbolically release those feelings of anger and disappointment to move on with your life.

- Get a pinata and whack it a few times, or join a boxing class. Anger, very similarly to stress, will manifest itself in a host of ways that can impact your mental state, or make you feel on edge. While I don't condone fighting, taking an organized martial arts class might be what you need to rid your body of that pent-up energy.

- Try a breathwork class. Breathwork is a kind of therapy that uses breathing exercises to improve mental clarity and spiritual health.

- Go hang out with animals. After my divorce I was raw with emotion, and it was hard for me to open up to people. Hanging out with animals was extremely therapeutic and allowed me to explore non-verbal communication as a form of expression. I was also able to verbalize my feelings to a captive audience without judgement. I know it sounds crazy, but it gave me the space I needed to hear my thoughts out loud, and it satisfied my need to be heard. Another option might be to get into a goat yoga class, or go horseback riding. You might find that you're surprisingly clearer and more trusting afterwards.

- Go hang out with that friend that's always over-excited to see you. Sometimes when you're so used to being drained, you forget what it feels like to be appreciated and loved. Hanging with someone who genuinely loves and respects you might help you replenish your emotional reserves.

- Go to a conference or event that feeds your soul. I don't know about you, but I always feel like I'm super pumped when I'm surrounded by like-minded individuals. There's something about sitting in a room of people who have faced similar life experiences as you that welcomes empowerment and validation.

- Create a vision board. This is typically a practice that people consider at the top of the year, but there's no rule that says you can't get clear about your life path in mid-March. Get some magazines, a poster board, some fun scissors, and get to it girlfriend!

- Create something with your hands. There's something about working with your hands that brings unimaginable clarity, calmness, and focus. If you live near a flower market, go get some flowers and make an arrangement. If baking is your thing, get on Pinterest, find an interesting recipe, and bake the day away.

- Pick a random Groupon and go do it. Kayaking classes anyone? Groupon, ClassPass, and a number of other discount websites offer tons of things to do at reasonable prices. Pick something that will push you a little out of your comfort zone, and go do it.

These are just a few ideas. But you get my drift. Find something weird, radical, or outside of the box to do by yourself. In addition to quality time alone, you'll also start to build a trove of new memories that will make for great conversation at cocktail parties and networking events. I mean seriously, how cool would it be to tell a bunch of strangers that you hang out with about horse-riding and pinatas that are all in the name of your mental health? It may not get you a whole lot of friends, but I guarantee it will help you find the right ones.

Put a Self-Care Plan into Practice

To determine what your plan of action looks like, you need to take some time to think about the things that might be red flags or early indicators that you need some self-care time. Below is an exercise that will help you gain clarity about the things you need to consider when it comes to your Self-Care Plan.

Instructions

I want you to grab a piece of paper and set it up with the following questions. Once you've set it up, answer each question honestly. Once you complete it, try to stick to it. Feel free to get an accountability buddy to help you stay on track. Repeat this process on a monthly or quarterly process.

My Self Care Plan

Which dates will I prioritize self-care in the next month or quarter?

_____

_____

Depressed to Daring

_____

_____

What is my budget for each day that I prioritize self-care?

_____

_____

_____

_____

What areas of my personal or professional life will I think about or evaluate on my self-care dates?

_____

_____

_____

_____

Will I use my self-care dates to spend time with a support group, therapist, friends or by myself? And if so, who will I spend each date I've committed to with?

_____

_____

_____

_____

Depressed to Daring

What is my intention for doing self-care this month?

_____

_____

_____

Are there any triggers or high-stress situations that are coming up this month or quarter that may require me to be more vigilant about self-care?

_____

_____

_____

What are some foods that will help me relax on the dates I've set for my self care?

_____

_____

_____

What are some take-aways I want to gain on my self care days?

_____

Depressed to Daring

_____

_____

_____

Words of affirmation to consider on days when I feel depleted are:

Whether you decide you want to commit to a plan that requires you to set aside 2 days a month or 20, your plan should be something you can see yourself doing for the long-haul. Over-committing may lead to burnout if you aren't careful. Look for ways you can be consistent. You should also put these dates on a calendar once you've committed to them. Set aside the money to complete them as well, don't wait for the day to roll around and discover you don't have the resources to spend time with yourself. The more you prioritize yourself, the higher the chance you'll see obvious positive outcomes from your self-care routine.

IN CASE NO ONE HAS TOLD YOU:

It is okay to take a break. It is not selfish to set boundaries around your happiness. It is okay to approach your life differently than what has been modeled for you by your parents or family. You are most empowered when you stand in your authentic truth, honoring that part of you that wants to show up for your deepest desires.

CHAPTER FIVE

ALIGN TO CLIMB

"Alignment trumps everything. Stay off the subject that disturbs your alignment, and everything that you are about will come into alignment."

— *Abraham Hicks*

If you've heard of the concept of the Law of Attraction, then you've likely been introduced to the idea of alignment, the conscious act of staying in line with your desired outcome through your thoughts and behavior. According to this belief system, your conscious and unconscious thoughts dictate your reality. Essentially it means that if you have a goal, a wish, or desire, and you believe it to your core, and stay in alignment with achieving it, that it can be yours.

When it comes to your emotional and mental health, being in alignment would be managing your emotions in such a fashion that you stay out of your own way and manifest your dreams in waking life. With regards to emotional agility, it means having the wherewithal to not haul off and throw a tantrum when something doesn't go your way. It's learning how to stand your ground, even if you're alone. It's having the fortitude to deal with your emotions and take the inspired action that lines up with your end goal.

So, for example, let's say you have an idea you want to pitch to your colleagues about a marketing campaign. The problem is, a colleague—we'll call her Cindy—always cuts you off or tries to take credit for your work. Over time, you feel less and less motivated to contribute to group projects because you don't feel acknowledged or heard. Privately, you yearn for more acknowledgement from your peers, and even feel that you should be promoted for your keen attention to details and out-of-the-box thinking, which is actually a skillset Cindy lacks. The aligned action in this scenario would be to continue going to the meetings, pitching your ideas, and remaining visible to your boss and other higher ups.

Depressed to Daring

Climbing out of your toxic traits or belief patterns can be an arduous task, but by realigning with your desired outcome when you feel off track or imbalanced, you create a flow of energy through your willingness to take inspired, aligned actions, and realize the end goal. You see, alignment keeps you eligible for the outcome. Controlling your thoughts can be a form of alignment, in the same way that controlling your temper can be aligned action. Ultimately it boils down to your willingness to observe your thoughts and gently pull yourself out of negative patterns when you notice any form of shift that doesn't line up with whatever you are trying to secure in your life.

The alignment of which I speak is facilitated by a compass that guides us all back to our personal truths. This compass always points us to our truth north, redirecting us to love, authenticity, and compassion—both for ourselves and those around us. Every woman has experienced the limitlessness of peace, joy, and abundance at some point in her life, and when we tap into that flow of exuberant energy, we can connect more easily to the inspired action that should guide us, even when we're emotional. When we feel something we don't agree with, not only does our body react by clamming up, increasing our heartbeat or flushing our skin, but we also subconsciously emit a signal to the universe that creates a space of misalignment and contrast. That contrast highlights the absence of the thing that we want, acting like an indicator that the dial your alignment is lined up with isn't correct. It's much like a radio: you can only pick up certain stations when you turn the knob a certain way. You can sense your alignment or lack thereof, when an outside influence interrupts the frequency, preventing clear words or music from coming through.

If you experience someone who is being snippy with you at the grocery store, for example, you will become agitated partly in response to the person's actions, but more so because the circumstance births a desire to be treated fairly. Furthermore, If we see we have commitments on our calendar and we don't have enough time to honor them, we desire more time and less restriction.

Earlier in this book, we discussed belief systems that have governed our self-perception and the stories we've created about our existence. In this chapter, I want you to consider your own actions and whether or not they align with the life you want to live. I know this seems simple, but alignment is where I see a lot of people fall short. Alignment is a discipline that is typically tempered by contrast—not that there's anything inherently wrong with contrast. it's just that the feelings and emotions that arise from it can get thrown into the mix of emotional junk you're trying to sift through that needs to be thrown out.

> "Alignment begins with a constituency of one. These are the individuals whose substance is real, pure and non-negotiable... Our level of effectiveness, contribution and integrity of work and life are in direct correlation with our level of integration, self-actualization and total alignment for body, mind and spirit."
>
> — Kristin S. Kaufman

What Does Alignment Look Like?

You can search the internet for more information about what alignment is an isn't, but for me, alignment looks a lot like radical self-care. It looks like honoring the woman you are on the inside, by protecting your energy, your emotions, and your future on the outside. It is when you love yourself and the life you are building so much that you actively participate in its preservation. It is a feeling of confidence and respect in yourself that guides your decision-making in every area of your life.

It can be as simple as setting boundaries with toxic people, but it can also mean confronting your own self-sabotaging habits. Whether you are someone on a quest to be the CEO of a company, the founder of a tech startup, or even a state senator, it would behoove you to get a hold on the things that trigger you, and to evaluate the ways in which you approach leadership and power. Emotional agility gives us the license to exercise our right to hold space in the world, but alignment is the process one would take to achieve success in those environments.

I know there is a lot of information out there that suggests that getting into alignment is simply removing your attention from things that are displeasing. However, I would argue that there is a lot of value in being able to experience displeasing things and still remain grounded while maintaining your alignment. By choosing not to allow every thought that enters your head to have a place in the story of your life, you create the kind of unshakable grit and chutzpah that is beneficial to you in high-stress situations.

How Do I Know if I'm Out of Alignment?

Believe it or not, the universe is always working for our highest good, and when we stay in the energy and flow of harmony in our lives, we partner with the universe to create a life beyond our wildest imagination. If you allow it, the universe will naturally rid you of the things that do not line up with that you want. The problem for most of us is that when we start losing things, or when we experience a shake-up in our life, we see it as a challenge, and we do everything we can to cling to things that are meant to be removed.

I think there's a misconception that happiness is only produced when things go right. But the truth is that our understanding of happiness is only created through the instability of contrast that appears in our lives when shit hits the fan. Yes, sometimes alignment is about focusing on the "good vibes," and positive things, but more often than not, it's about the expansion that happens on an emotional or mental level when we are pushed beyond our comfort zones.

Being in alignment is being in the flow. It's allowing things to leave or fall away when they need to. It's allowing yourself to take the information you gain from the experience of loss and consciously transforming it into wisdom.

When you are not in the flow, you create resistance, and more often than not, a lot of problems for yourself in the process. You will know that you're out of alignment because either A, your body will tell you and you'll have a gut reaction that something is off, or B, when you become self-aware enough to realize that a lot of your problems are self-inflicted and could have been avoided through acute discipline.

Depressed to Daring

Your Gut Gives Guidance

Have you ever had a feeling that something was off about a person, place, or thing, and you just absolutely knew what you were feeling was true, despite having no evidence that you were correct? That feeling is your intuition providing you guidance about something that should either be avoided altogether or examined further. It is something that is formed by your belief system and cultivated by the thoughts and feelings you've adopted as your foundation since birth. For this reason, the feeling that is emitted from your body when it is triggered is so specific to you, that others cannot weigh in on what you're experiencing. They can only tell you if they too have been alarmed by their own gut, or if they have information that might validate your perspective.

When it comes to emotional agility, your gut can give you a heads up that certain outcomes might be more probable than others. In the same way that a warning light comes on before you run out of gas, your gut alerts you to the fact that by continuing on a certain course of action, without considering the information that it's feeding you, you might run out of gas or experience an unfortunate series of events.

I don't mean to sound too glib, though. Yes, your gut will alert you when things aren't quite right, but they also let you know whether or not you are in alignment with the energy that keeps you in flow with your highest good. Let's say you have to deliver a huge presentation on behalf of your company, but the night before, your girlfriends invite you out. At one point, you run into an old crush, and you hit it off. Before you know it, it's 1 a.m., you're slightly tipsy, and still chatting at the bar even though you need to be up by 6 a.m. to get ready. I can pretty much guarantee that your stomach will start to hurt, or that some other painful nudge will occur, and worsen until you get up and go home.

Like any muscle in the body, the gut must be developed. In order to do this, you have to get into the habit of listening for the nudges, acting on them, and learning to protect yourself with the information you are receiving. By doing so, you stay in alignment with the positive outcome that your subconscious is guiding you towards.

Align to Level Up

There is a force of energy that dwells within you that is so powerful it can affect your environment. In the same way that your brain produces the energy that sparks movement to your limbs and pumps blood throughout your body, it also emits brain waves, or vibrations, which can be measured in frequencies. Leveling up, in business and in life, occurs when the frequencies that are emitted by your brain line up with the harmony produced by your thoughts and actions.

The key to climbing from lower vibrations to higher, more fulfilling frequencies is to focus your energy on the things that line up with the outcome. Vibrational energy also happens to increase as levels of emotional energy increase as well, making it easier to draw things to you solely by your disciplined focus. In this book we've discussed the Law of Cause and Effect, and I briefly touched on the concept of the Law of Attraction earlier in this chapter. For those of you who don't know, the Law of Attraction is the magnetic power the universe uses to draw similar energies together.

Depressed to Daring

When you shift your attention from being resistant to an event to open and accepting, you can attract or magnetize events, circumstances, and people into your life that will produce an outcome based on the corresponding energy. So, if you want a raise, and you keep your thoughts focused, yet malleable, and stay in a grounded place while you navigate, it can be yours.

Your brain is always releasing energy into the world, and therefore it is constantly drawing things to you by your thoughts and actions. So, when your mind is focused on progress, abundance, growth, and expansion, and your actions do not form resistance to it, you will draw prosperity and opportunity into your life over time.

In order to align yourself, you just need to try your best to be tuned into the energy that produces outcomes that are in your highest good.

While alignment is the bridge between who you are as person today and the life you want to experience, there are a few tools you can use like affirmations, meditation and visualization to help you get clear on the things you are hoping to see unfold in your life.

Affirmations for Alignment

Affirmations are short, positive statements that you can say to yourself to help you overcome negative self-talk, limiting beliefs or self-sabotaging thought cycles. The idea is to recite the statements to yourself at least once a day, or anytime you find yourself lost in negative thinking. So for example, if you find yourself ruminating on something that was negative or

Depressed to Daring

hurtful in your past, you would recite an affirmation to yourself to seemingly divert your attention away from the negativity, to something positive about yourself. By doing this often, you can start to create positive thought cycles for you to focus on. You would then align your behavior to match the affirmation and re-ground yourself in a more positive mindset.

In addition to helping you to divert your attention back to the positive aspects of your life, you can use them as mini springboards for visualization and meditation.

You can recite these out loud anywhere, at any time of day. To get the maximum effect however, I would suggest setting aside 15-20 minutes each day to affirm positive thoughts to yourself.

Here are 20 to get you started.

1. I am capable of amazing things.
2. I am not my parents.
3. I accept all choices I've made as the best decisions I could make with the knowledge and information I had at the time.
4. I understand that I have the power to change my life.
5. I know everything is always working out for my highest good.
6. I turn down the volume on my inner critic. I extend my energy in the direction of that which best serves me.
7. I honor my truth, and I invite those that honor my truth into my life.
8. I stand in my truth, my whole truth and nothing but my truth.
9. I know am lovable.
10. I am doing the best I can with the information and resources available to me.

Depressed to Daring

11. I am a powerful, confident, emotionally grounded woman.
12. I am a work in progress.
13. I'm aloud to live my life in the best way I see fit.
14. I do not owe anyone my shame.
15. I am able to discern how to react in situations where I feel overwhelmed.
16. I can shift my thoughts to joy, abundance and contentment at any time.
17. I am on a journey to self-actualization. I'm aloud to examine and re-examine what I believe to be true about myself.
18. I exude joy and happiness.
19. I am the creator of my own thoughts.
20. I can manifest a life beyond my wildest dreams.

The Value in Visualization

Using visualization as a technique to focus your emotional attention can be a powerful way to establish alignment on a day-to-day basis. In terms of alignment, visualization is the action of creating a clear picture of what you want in your head and staying in a balanced emotional space to receive it. More specifically, it's having the discipline to imagine everything you've ever wanted coming to you. The idea is to see what you want to happen in your life so vividly that you feel the emotions of excitement and elation that would come upon its arrival.

And last, but certainly not least, you can also leverage the power of meditation to get clear.

Meditation

Depressed to Daring

Meditation is the habitual process of training your mind to focus and redirect your thoughts. You can leverage it to do several things, but for the sake of this conversation, you would use it to increase awareness about yourself, your circumstances and your surroundings. During meditation, activity in your parietal lobe, *which processes sensory information and gives us an understanding spatial our orientation and awareness of our body*, slows down to a trickle. While it is in this slowed state, you can sit or lay down, and focus your attention on the things you want to see come into your life. In addition to an increase of clarity, there are also other benefits like reduced stress, a stronger attention span, lighten your mood, and even help you curb cravings and addictions.

Meditation gives you the opportunity to freeze frame memories, scenarios and thoughts so that you can view them from multiple angles and take note of the feelings and emotions associated with those things.

IN CASE NO ONE HAS TOLD YOU:

You are the only one who receives the guidance from your gut. You and you alone are responsible for following it, and you do not owe anyone an explanation for following the non-physical nudges of advice you are receiving from your subconscious.

To trust your gut is to trust yourself. And by doing so, you create confidence and self-respect for your personal values and belief system.

CHAPTER SIX

PURGE TO RE-EMERGE

"Edit your life frequently and ruthlessly. It's your masterpiece after all."

— *N. W. Morris*

If we are being brutally honest, most of us have probably needed a good purge at some point in our lives. Whether the need developed due to the stress that came with life changes like birth, death, marriage, divorce, or from professional pressures like job loss, change in career, or even switching industries, the heap of feelings that you've had to navigate during these times could have been overwhelming. And unless you have a plan to purge yourself of what is being bottled up in situations like these, you'll likely drown in a sea of emotions if things go unaddressed for too long.

Catharsis (aka "emotional purging") is a process that can help you eliminate emotions that don't serve you. Being able to rid ourselves of the feelings of guilt, shame, inadequacy, and anger associated with whatever we are experiencing can help us release the heaviness of our experiences. It's important to point out that catharsis isn't really meant to end all of our suffering; it's about getting in touch with our inner truth. In doing so, we can escape submersion from the abyss of our emotions. Purging, like any other act of clearing, allows us to rearrange the way we view our experiences—but only once we clear up enough space to do so. It's the action we must take once we've identified the information that doesn't support the new story we are telling about our lives. We also get to energetically release the things that have blocked our ability to grow.

So, if we can clearly see how beneficial it can be, why is it so doggone hard to actually do?

I'll tell you why: it's because our ego is fearful that we will mistakenly toss out something we may need later. And instead of trusting ourselves—that we've made the correct decision to support our mental and emotional health—we try to buy ourselves time to figure out if we have, in fact, acted in our own best interest. I would also argue, as was the case with me, that sometimes we don't purge because, deep down, we know that purging isn't an instant fix. We know that once we bring those feelings to the surface, all bets are off, and we aren't quite sure if we want to stick around for what happens next.

And who can blame you, right? I mean seriously, is there ever a great time to deal with the emotions you've repressed about feeling unloved or unheard since you were eight? The issue, though, is that sooner or later our avoidance behaviors catch up with us. Because when we run from the truth—and let's face it: most people do—we spend our energy protecting the very anger, strife, stress, and pain that are preventing us from being set free. All we need to do is take a step back and look at the bigger picture. If we don't purge, the negative energy will fester and manifest itself in our behavior, resulting in the desire to get even, seek revenge, or sabotage ourselves through drug and alcohol abuse

Now, I don't know what your traumas are, or what baggage you've been secretly carrying throughout your life, but I will say this: purging is a lot like taking out the trash. When you take the trash out of your house, the place feels better, looks cleaner, and you can see the things inside your home more easily—not to mention access them. You wouldn't go years (or even weeks) without taking the trash from your physical space, so why are you keeping it in your emotional space? And what do you have to gain from doing so?

The harsh reality is that if you want to live your best life, you're going to have to cut through your own BS, and get to the heart of the matter—whatever is preventing you from living free of toxicity. I realize this is not an easy process, but it can be hugely transformative if you allow it.

Some things to remember throughout the process:

- You are not responsible for others' perception of you.
- You are not the sum of your toxic past behaviors.
- You are not weak for needing or wanting to deal with your emotions.
- Avoiding the purge to escape feelings of sadness is a grave error.
- There's no timeline for you to have everything filled out.
- Our fears and trauma have a sneaky way of making us feel isolated, vulnerable, and embarrassed. This is normal, but as you do the work you will release the need to be victimized by these feelings.

When we consider the life experiences we've had, especially in instances when we felt powerless, defeated, betrayed or depressed, it can be like ripping a soft scab off of a tender wound. Showing up for the purge will be one of the bravest things you'll ever do, but it won't look like it at first. Purging will, over time, allow you to let go of the things that don't belong in your story, but until this occurs, it's important to keep yourself moving forward and actively working through the issues.

In today's world, purging, or actively releasing toxic beliefs, stories, and thoughts is essential to obtaining, and maintaining emotional groundedness, especially if you are in a position of power. I don't care if these people are your employees, or your kids, they deserve the most grounded, agile version of you. They deserve the you that won't be triggered by your own demons when it's time to take action or deal with a person whom you don't like. They deserve the leader in you that can discern the right time to speak up for a cause, mission, or group—the same leader who is grounded enough to hold her tongue when confronted with uncomfortable news or circumstances.

So, what does purging look like?

Well, in addition to self-care, purging in real life looks like therapy with a licensed therapist or a counselor (trained professional, pastor, life coach, etc.), speaking to friends and family, or working through your issues with a Surrender Circle.

Therapy

I know therapy is a touchy subject for a lot of people. I'm keenly aware that cultural or religious beliefs, familial attitudes, or just the simple fact that it's considered taboo, makes it difficult to discuss amongst your peers or colleagues. But since I've benefited from therapy, and because I now see how going helped me to be more grounded and impactful in my personal and professional life, I feel like it's my duty to tell you what you stand to gain by going. My goal isn't to guilt you into going, but to open your eyes to the possibilities that open up for you, especially if you've ever experienced some kind of life-changing or traumatic event.

So, here's my story.

In February 2017, I delivered my son, Aiden, roughly six weeks early. The night I went into the hospital was like any other night. I made pappardelle Bolognese for dinner. I had an episode

Depressed to Daring

of *Game of Thrones* locked and loaded on the TV. My older two kids had been fed, and I had just started to dig into my meal when I got a call from the nurse unit at Kaiser San Francisco. Earlier in the day I had called them to complain about some cramping and swelling.

Although they had told me that I could come in and get monitored several hours earlier, I'd figured I was just experiencing Braxton Hicks contractions and decided to stay home. I had already been through two natural births and was well versed on how the visits to the hospital go when they need to monitor you. You go there, waste five hours, lie uncomfortably in bed with no snack or Wi-Fi, and then you feel like you should have just stayed home.

But I digress. In this case, the nurse was concerned and was following up to ask me to come in, just to double check that it wasn't something more serious. Reluctantly, I decided to leave my half-eaten dinner on the table and drive to San Francisco from Pacifica, California. Once we got there, they took me upstairs right away. They ran some tests, asked me some routine questions and then the nurses disappeared for more than awhile. It was so long, that I started to get suspicious, so I finally alerted them to come to my room by pushing the call-button situated on my hospital bed.

No response.

What seemed like more than five minutes went by, and I pressed it again, and finally a doctor emerged. He informed me that I my blood pressure was dangerously high, and that I was in the danger zone for a condition called Preeclampsia. Preeclampsia can develop without warning and progress quickly. If left unaddressed for too long, it can result in additional delivery complications and/or death for the infant and mother. They said the only way to prevent the complications from getting worse was to induce and deliver.

So, I have to tell you: at this point, I was absolutely scared out of my mind. Not for myself, but I was terrified that something was going to happen to my baby. For this reason, I agreed to the new birth plan. We induced labor, and within a few hours Aiden was born at five pounds even. Despite the change in plans, I figured the worst was behind me. I knew that my son would have to go to the NICU for a few days, but figured for the most part we'd be in clear to go home in the coming weeks.

This was partially true. As it turned out, the delivery didn't prevent my blood pressure from soaring even higher, nor did it prevent post-partum pre-eclampsia from developing. In a matter of days, I went from being optimistic that my baby would be able to come home with me, to having him cleared to leave the NICU while I stayed under the close care of a team of doctors who were working around the clock to bring my blood pressure down.

It was an absolute mess, and my emotions, predictably, were all over the place. I just wanted to go home. And I got pretty close to getting cleared after being there for five days, until the unimaginable happened.

I was lying in bed on my back with my eyes open when I started to get the most painful migraine I had ever felt in my life. The pain went from mild to severe in a matter of seconds. At the same time, my vision blurred, and the things that had

Depressed to Daring

been in focus only moments earlier dissolved into mirage waves, engulfing the room. And then, without warning, I felt suffocated, like all the in my body was being drawn out against my will. This caused the migraine to intensify as the pressure built. But most notably, my chest was on fire. It felt like someone was repeatedly pressing me with a scalding hot cast iron pan. As all of this was happening, I was able to shriek, "Help!" Although I couldn't see, I heard the gallop of a thousand footsteps racing towards my room. There was commotion and indistinct yelling amongst the doctors. The room filled up with medical staff. I didn't know what was happening, but I could feel my essence and my lifeforce being taken from my body, and that's when I started to recite the Lord's Prayer in my mind.

I couldn't move my mouth or any of my limbs.

I couldn't breathe. The pressure in my head was unbearable.

From the right side of the room I heard my nurse yell, "Code Blue!" I remember thinking, *Is this the end?* Was I going to die at 32? **And then everything went silent.**

"He who has health, has hope; and he who has hope, has everything."
- Thomas Carlyle

While there are a lot of benefits of speaking to a close friend after a traumatic or life-changing event, there are some things that even our closest friends cannot really help us to reconcile. And quite honestly, for our own sake and for theirs, it's not completely fair to put them in a situation where they have to help you navigate through experiences that you don't even have a grasp on yet. Talking to a therapist can help you sift through the details of your experiences that you wouldn't have considered on your own, and they can even help you identify patterns and synchronicities within your behavior.

A great therapist can help you figure out ways you can cope after loss, or even help you create a plan of action to help you purge or eliminate harmful habits, thoughts and ideas that you would likely struggle with on your own. They can also help you find balance while you are purging, so you don't go too deep too many days in a row.

After suffering a mini-stroke and experiencing a near-death experience after the birth of my third child, I took myself to see a therapist. I was struggling to make sense of the emotions I'd experienced in the hospital. I knew I wanted a logical explanation for what happened, but I also needed to explore questions about the meaning of life, including why and how I survived, without being judged. Having a therapist gave me the opportunity to explore those questions without placing that burden on friends and family. It also took me off the hook of feeling like I needed to figure everything out by myself.

I'm not sure where the thinking began that if we just push through and deal with things privately, they'll eventually go away or get better, but this is a shortsighted belief that doesn't account for the amount of work that is truly required to dismantle your habits and heighten your own sense of self-awareness.

Depressed to Daring

What's unfortunate is that most people wait until their entire world is ablaze to go and seek help. They wait until things are nearly unmanageable and then show up, expecting a miracle therapist to address issues that have been entrenched for far too long. Ladies, I can assure you that while the therapist will help you to examine challenging areas of your life, no one wields a magic wand to make all issues disappear. You have the power to transform anything in your life, and you don't have to wait until you're depleted to get guidance. You also don't need to experience a huge life event to justify getting a therapist. I would actually encourage you to regularly talk to someone about small things in your life so they don't become larger down the road. Some therapists specialize in certain disciplines, but there are actually a lot of things that a therapist might be able to help you work through like:

- Depression and anxiety
- Issues with adjusting to new circumstances.
- Repeated issues in romantic relationships
- Addiction
- Codependency
- Moodiness
- Eating disorders
- Body dysmorphia
- Self-harm
- Grief
- Infertility
- Marriage
- Anger issues
- Fear
- Issues with toxic parents
- Your sexuality
- Your gender identity
- Your racial or ethnic identity

What to Look for in a Good Therapist or Counselor

Over the years, I've come to know a lot of women who have opted to change their lives for the better with the guidance of a therapist. I've also had my own experiences with therapy and have learned a lot about what does and doesn't work for myself and my larger network—key factors in selecting a therapist. I say *select* purposely, because you should be *empowered* to play an active part in your mental health by selecting the person you feel you'll enjoy the most positive outcomes with. It is important to remember that a therapist is a partner and an ally for your health and wellbeing; they are *not a friend*. They are there to help you make sense of your emotions as related to difficult situations.

Unless you've received a reputable referral from a friend, chances are your first could of visits will be an opportunity to get to know the therapist, and to get a sense of whether or not you want to partner with them. Here are seven things to consider during those initial visits:

1. *Do they have interpersonal skills?* In those first few visits ask yourself, are they good communicators? Do they show a sense of understanding and warmth? Can they pick up on your non-verbal cues and give guidance based on all of the information you are giving to them, whether it's spoken or not?

2. *Do you really trust them?* Is this someone you feel would have your best interest at heart? Do you believe they have any bias that could impact how they will manage your sessions? If you find either of these things questionable, then it might not be a good fit.

3. *Can they offer a clear explanation of your symptoms and treatment plan?* When I sought therapeutic partnership after the difficult birth of my son, it was imperative for me to understand why I was feeling certain things, and I wanted clear guidance from the therapist about a plan of action that would help to bring my emotions into balance. A good therapist should be able to tell you what they believe you are symptomatic of and let you know what their course of treatment will look like.

4. *Do they make you feel hopeful that you can improve your life with their assistance?* There's nothing more dreadful than working up the nerve to seek a therapist, and coughing up the dough for assistance, only to find yourself beaten down, feeling uninspired by a mediocre therapist. I'm not saying they need to feed you false hope that everything will be fine, but you should leave your appointments feeling generally optimistic that you got something out of going.

5. *Are they knowledgeable about your cultural background, religious beliefs, gender, or sexual orientation?* Simply put, do they know how to give guidance that might be in alignment with your value system? For example, if you are struggling with coming out, or making a decision to divorce, ask yourself, would it make sense to see someone who has views, religious or not, that might impact their ability to effectively guide you without their own bias? I can't begin to tell you the number of people I've run into who feel like their therapist doesn't get them or their cultural background. There's no sense in wasting more time and money to get the same feedback. Empower yourself to find a therapeutic partner that's going to be cognizant of certain factors in your life without you taking

an entire session to educate them. Life is too short, and money doesn't grow on trees. Get a therapist that "gets you!"

6. *Are they abreast of recent research evidence?* You need to know if they are up to date on the latest techniques and standards in their industry. You need to know if they are providing you with guidance that is in accordance with the latest standards.

7. *Are they committed to being the best therapist or counselor they can be?* All licensed professionals must participate in some kind of continuing education program to maintain their credentials—by law. But, even so, you need to get clarity about what they've done to go a step beyond the bare minimum. Do they attend conferences regularly? Are they a published author? Are they highly respected? Do other mental health and wellness professionals generally share their same view? Having this insight early in your working relationship will help you manage your expectations for the kind of guidance you are likely to receive. It also lets you know if they are best suited for you and a treatment plan that you could commit to in the long term.

Surrender Circles

A Surrender Circle is a group of individuals who are committed to helping each other support their mental health. The people in the group act as accountability buddies and are there to allow each other to surrender challenges or issues they are facing in a safe emotional space. Additionally, a Surrender Circle helps the participants maintain a sense of accountability to a committed self-care routine and mental health. The group can be as small as two people or as large as one hundred. The size isn't necessarily important, but what is is having trustworthy participants involved—ones that will help to maintain confidentiality. It's kind of hard to expect one hundred people to be completely confidential about what happens in the group, but if you're willing to draft up an ironclad NDA, go for it.

Very similar to seeing a therapist regularly, you'd stay in contact with your circle over an extended period of time. You can also commit to reading or studying certain books, as well as performing certain exercises to help you purge your emotions in a safe space. The goal of the group is to help you surrender things that are keeping you down. You would share your experiences with each other, and you'd plan outings, which could be self-care events, together. You could also use the group to do some pretty radical emotional work. For example, you could have a Purge Party where you do some verbal vomit exercises as a group. The verbal vomit exercises are based on role play, where the vomiter/purger purges, or expresses their feelings for a set amount of time. Think of it as a Twitter rant, except you get to speak your thoughts aloud, uninterrupted, and you don't have a character cap for your thoughts.

Verbal Vomit Exercises

Verbal vomit can be an effective tool to help you eliminate your raw emotions. Whether you need to air your feelings about relationship drama, your in-laws, bill collectors, or your boss, verbal vomit gets the gunk out of your emotional space.

Here's how it works:
1. Two people stand across from each other. One person will purge and the other will be an active listener.

2. The purger informs the listener of what they need to release and the amount of time they feel they'll need to talk for.
3. The listener sets the clock and lets the purger know when it's okay to begin. Once the purger starts, the listener becomes responsible for timekeeping and encouragement to the purger. Encouragement would be saying things like, "Is that all? Or, how did that make you feel?"
4. When the time is up, the listener stops the purger from going further, and they speak words of support and affirmation to the purger. To be clear, support and affirmation shouldn't be expressed as ill wishes or negativity against whatever or whomever the purger was discussing. All feedback should relate specifically to the purger.

Ridding ourselves of the thoughts, feelings, and emotions that don't serve us is tough work. It's not meant to be easy or brief. It's meant to be rewarding, though. If you've ever experienced some level of anxiety, depression, or even isolation because you don't feel like you have anyone you can talk to, then you know what it feels like to be submerged in the fear that things can't or won't get better.

Purging, talking, and relating with one another frees us to become stronger, more agile versions of ourselves. If we can just learn to lean into the suck of situations that don't always make us feel warm and fuzzy, we can establish a foundation that accounts for the curve balls that life will inevitably throw at us. Releasing our fears and choosing to have faith in the women we evolve into as we learn to respect the language of our emotions not only allows us to take our power back but re-emerge as powerful women, mothers, leaders, and change-agents.

We can change the trajectory of our lives by being mindful about our mental health.

We can change the landscape for each other by modeling behavior that teaches the next generation of women to get gritty and agile when things don't go our way.

It is empowering to partner with therapists, counselors, and life coaches as a way to support our health as we pursue our wildest dreams.

We can redefine what success looks like for women by creating an expanded vision for achievement that acknowledges the importance of emotional agility, mental health, and self-care.

We just have to get radical!

And I believe we can.

Are you with me?

IN CASE NO ONE HAS TOLD YOU:

You are loved. You are joy.
You are excitement in motion.

You will move mountains.
You will change lives.
You will get that promotion.

You will find support.
You will break cycles of self-doubt.
You will find your voice.

In Conclusion

> "This is why alchemy exists," the boy said. "So that everyone will search for his treasure, find it, and then want to be better than he was in his former life. Lead will play its role until the world has no further need for lead; and then lead will have to turn itself into gold. That's what alchemists do. They show that, when we strive to become better than we are, everything around us becomes better, too."
>
> — Paulo Coelho, The Alchemist

In the time it took me to live through the experiences described in this book, and to be disciplined enough to sit down and get them on paper, I've come to accept two things: What we believe about ourselves sets the tone for every possibility that manifests in our lives. When we show up for our own transformation, we can improve the quality of those around us in a way that's both powerful and significant.

As women in this day in age, we are already aware of how significant and important it is for us to hold space in environments we occupy, but now is the time to learn how to be more strategic. It is no longer enough to know we need to break glass ceilings. It's not enough to dream about what is possible. Now is the time to get really honest about what our mental and emotional health must encompass, to not only shatter the ceiling, but to thrive once we are on the other side.

Depressed to Daring

It is through our commitment to fully valuing and appreciating ourselves, even the parts that we have not always been proud of, that we reinvent the norm for women around the world. We do not have to sacrifice our minds, our health or our bodies in order to gain respect. When we start from a place of self-respect, it becomes possible to sacrifice anxiety and depression to gain freedom and the success that we seek. As we focus our attention on how we think and how we set boundaries in our lives, we will also empower the next generation of women to take better care of themselves. Being a daring, confident, emotionally grounded woman means having the confidence to know that I have the fortitude and the tools to experience a storm without being completely shaken by it. As I evaluate my own life, and the things that used to overtake me, I can honestly say that there's nothing more fulfilling than knowing that I don't have to be that anxiety-ridden, fearful depressed person any more. I have the power to be the fearless, badass, trail blazer that I've always known on the inside. And I believe, through your decision to show up for your life, and take control of your thoughts and how you allow them to impact you, that you can too!

Acknowledgements

Writing a book was not only therapeutic but it turned out to be more rewarding than I could have ever imagined. Thank you to my brother Adam, who has shown me what true love is and who has inspired me to speak my truth and own every inch of who I am. Thank you to Minnie, for being the best sister I could have ever prayed for.

To coach Dan Luna: thank you for taking a chance on a hard-headed girl from Pasadena. You never made me feel like I was difficult and never made me feel unvalidated. You just saw an athlete that needed a little guidance and support to grow into her best self. Thank you.

I'm eternally grateful to **Christina Harbridge**, who inspired me to challenge the beliefs I had about myself, and armed me with the idea that I could be a better leader, a better mother, and a better person by understanding and accepting the language of my emotions.

Finally, to all those who have been a part of my getting here: my brothers Chuckie Shaw, Shawn Shaw and Jason Shaw, my sister-in-law Melissa Shaw, my bonus mother Pat Banks, Dan and Lori Derkum, Rami and Adi Demirovic, Mika and David Mc.Griff, Mom, and to my father . . . thank you for your encouragement, love, and never-ending support.

About the Author

Adonica is a 3x TEDx speaker, author, and marketing professional with years of experience in business development and strategic partnerships.

She has been a weather woman, a Division I athlete, a contestant on a dating show, and she's even run for office. She's a pilot in training. She's survived appendicitis, an appendectomy, a divorce, and the loss of her childhood dreams—twice.

She fancies herself a bit of an "Adversity Expert," and has a longstanding history of dealing with difficult sh*! in the face of depression and anxiety.

In *Depressed to Daring*, she discusses the secrets to her success and how she's been able to beat depression and anxiety despite everything life has thrown her way.

In parallel, she teaches women on how to manage stress and anxiety through radical self-care, mindfulness, and emotional agility.

Follow Adonica on
Instagram @adonicashaw and
Facebook @adonicamshaw2

CPSIA information can be obtained
at www.ICGtesting.com
Printed in the USA
LVHW041048170220
647167LV00017B/227/J